Worldwide Acclaim for Sudoku

"Diabolically addictive."
　—*New York Post*

T0286673

"A puzzling global phenomenon."
　—*The Economist*

"The biggest craze to hit *The Times* since the first crossword puzzle was published in 1935."
　—*The Times* of London

"The latest craze in games."
　—BBC News

"Sudoku is dangerous stuff. Forget work and family—think papers hurled across the room and industrial-sized blobs of correction fluid. I love it!"
　—*The Times* of London

"Sudoku are to the first decade of the twenty-first century what Rubik's Cube was to the 1970s."
　—*The Daily Telegraph*

"Britain has a new addiction. Hunched over newspapers on crowded subway trains, sneaking secret peeks in the office, a puzzle-crazy nation is trying to slot numbers into small checkerboard grids."
　—Associated Press

"Forget crosswords."
　—*The Christian Science Monitor*

Also Available

Sudoku Easy Presented by Will Shortz, Volume 1

Sudoku Easy to Hard Presented by Will Shortz, Volume 2

Sudoku Easy to Hard Presented by Will Shortz, Volume 3

The Ultimate Sudoku Challenge Presented by Will Shortz

Sudoku for Your Coffee Break Presented by Will Shortz

For Sudoku Lovers: 300 Puzzles in Just One Book!

The Giant Book of Sudoku Presented by Will Shortz

Try These Convenient, Portable Volumes

Pocket Sudoku Presented by Will Shortz, Volume 1

Pocket Sudoku Presented by Will Shortz, Volume 2

SUDOKU

TO BOOST YOUR BRAINPOWER

PRESENTED BY WILL SHORTZ
100 WORDLESS CROSSWORD PUZZLES

EDITED BY
WILL SHORTZ

PUZZLES BY
PZZL.COM

ST. MARTIN'S GRIFFIN
NEW YORK

www.stmartins.com

ISBN 0-312-35814-8
EAN 978-0-312-35814-3

Introduction

If you're like most sudoku solvers, when you're stymied (at least temporarily) by a sudoku, you wonder, "Am I missing something . . . or is something wrong with this puzzle?"

I can *say* each puzzle in this book is guaranteed to have a unique answer. Maybe you'll believe me.

I can also *say* you'll never need to guess to complete any puzzle here. Every one can be solved using step-by-step logic. No testing of hypotheses is necessary.

Still, it's one thing to make these claims and another thing entirely to back them up.

Now, for the first time in any sudoku book, we're providing complete, step-by-step explanations for selected puzzle solutions (immediately following puzzle #100). The eight solutions we picked to explain are the first two puzzles in each of the first three sections—Light and Easy, Moderate, and Demanding—and the first and last puzzles in the final section, Beware! Very Challenging! Among these, all the basic solving strategies, and most of the advanced ones as well, are illustrated.

Each explanation gives in straightforward English one way to complete the puzzle. Your own reasoning, of course, may differ, and any way you get to the solution is fine.

There wasn't room to provide explanations for all one hundred puzzles in this book. But if you can master all the techniques explained here, you will also be able to do all the puzzles whose solutions aren't explained, as well as virtually any sudoku anywhere else.

That's boosting your brainpower.

As in our companion volumes, all the puzzles herein were created by Peter Ritmeester and the staff of PZZL.com, an Internet technology company devoted to puzzles. Peter is the general secretary of the World Puzzle

Federation, an international body promoting language- and culture-neutral puzzles (like sudoku), of which he and I were cofounders in 1999. Peter's work appears in major publications and on Web sites throughout the world. Thanks to Nancy Schuster for help in preparing the manuscript.

Happy sudoku-ing!

—Will Shortz

How to Solve Sudoku

A sudoku puzzle consists of a 9 × 9–square grid subdivided into nine 3 × 3 boxes. Some of the squares contain numbers. The object is to fill in the remaining squares so that every row, every column, and every 3 × 3 box contains each of the numbers from 1 to 9 exactly once.

Solving a sudoku puzzle involves pure logic. No guesswork is needed—or even desirable. Getting started involves mastering just a few simple techniques.

Take the example on this page (in which we've labeled the nine 3 × 3 boxes A to I as shown). Note that the boxes H and I already have 8's filled in, but box G does not. Can you determine where the 8 goes here?

5	8	6					1	2
				5	2	8	6	
2	4		8	1				3
			5		3		9	
			8	1	2	4		
4		5	6			7	3	8
	5		2	3			8	1
7				8				
3	6			5				

A	B	C
D	E	F
G	H	I

The 8 can't appear in the top row of squares in box G, because an 8 already appears in the top row of I—and no number can be repeated in a row. Similarly, it can't appear in the middle row of G, because an 8 already appears in the middle row of H. So, by process of elimination, an 8 must appear in the bottom row of G. Since only one square in this row is empty—next to the 3 and 6—you have your first answer. Fill in an 8 to the right of the 6.

Next, look in the three left-hand boxes of the grid, A, D, and G. An 8 appears in both A and G (the latter being the one you just entered). In box A, the 8 appears in the middle column, while in G the 8 appears on the right. By elimination, in box D, an 8 must go in the leftmost column. But which square? The column here has two squares open.

The answer is forced by box E. Here an 8 appears in the middle row. This means an 8 cannot appear in the middle row of D. Therefore, it must appear in the top row of the leftmost column of D. You have your second answer.

In solving a sudoku, build on the answers you've filled in as far as possible—left, right, up, and down—before moving on.

For a different kind of logic, consider the sixth row of numbers— 4, ?, 5, 6, ?, ?, 7, 3, 8. The missing numbers must be 1, 2, and 9, in some order. The sixth square can't be a 1, because box E already has a 1. And it can't be a 2, because a 2 already appears in the sixth column in box B. So the sixth square in the sixth row has to be a 9. Fill this in.

Now you're left with just 1 and 2 for the empty squares of this row. The fifth square can't be a 1, because box E already has a 1. So the fifth square must be a 2. The second square, by elimination, has a 1. Voilà! Your first complete row is filled in.

Box E now has only two empty squares, so this is a good spot to consider next. Only the 4 and 7 remain to be filled in. The leftmost square of the middle row can't be a 4, because a 4 already appears in this row in box F. So it must be 7. The remaining square must be 4. Your first complete box is done.

One more tip, and then you're on your own.

Consider 3's in the boxes A, B, and C. Only one 3 is filled in—in the third row, in box C. In box A you don't have enough information to fill in a 3 yet. However, you know the 3 can't appear in A's bottom row, because 3 appears in the bottom row of C. And it can't appear in the top row, because that row is already done. Therefore, it must appear in the middle row. Which square you don't know yet. But now, by elimination, you do know that in box B a 3 must appear in the top row. Specifically, it must appear in the fourth column, because 3's already appear in the fifth and sixth columns of E and H. Fill this in.

Following logic, using these and other techniques left for you to discover, you can work your way around the grid, filling in the rest of the missing numbers. The complete solution is shown below.

5	8	6	3	7	4	9	1	2
1	3	7	9	5	2	8	6	4
2	4	9	8	1	6	5	7	3
8	7	2	5	4	3	1	9	6
6	9	3	7	8	1	2	4	5
4	1	5	6	2	9	7	3	8
9	5	4	2	3	7	6	8	1
7	2	1	4	6	8	3	5	9
3	6	8	1	9	5	4	2	7

Remember, don't guess. Be careful not to repeat a number where you shouldn't, because a wrong answer may force you to start over. And don't give up. Soon you'll be a sudoku master!

SUDOKU

TO BOOST YOUR BRAINPOWER

PRESENTED BY WILL SHORTZ

1 Light and Easy

		7				9		5
	5		1	9	7	3	8	
9	3			2		1		7
		9	5	8	4	2	1	3
		8	3	7				9
			6					8
	8	5	2		6			
4			7			6		
7	6	2	9	5		8	3	

1			7				8	4
3	2	4	8	1		5	7	
	5	8		4	9	1		
	4	6				7	1	
				8		6	3	
5	3		2		1			8
		1		3		2		
	7		1		4			3
				7	8	4		

		7	3	8				
	6				2	5		
2	4		7		5	8		3
9	8						5	
4	5	1	2			9	8	
	7			5	8	4		
8	3	5	1	6			2	
1	2		5	7		6	3	
		6						

	9				5	6		
	7			8		3		2
	5	3		6		8	9	
5	1	2	4				3	6
7			5				8	
9					1		2	5
1		7		5	9			3
3	2		6	4		5		
8	4							7

5   Light and Easy

7				9	8	6		
4		2	1		7			8
9	3				2			
		6	2	4			7	9
2			7				4	5
1	7	4	9	8			2	
6		7	8		9	4	5	
				7	6			
		5		1				7

	3	5	4	7	9	2	8	1
	8			6		3		7
					1			5
					8		2	3
			1	9	2	4		6
	2	7		3		8		
	1	3			7		9	4
7			8		6	5		
	6					7		8

	3			2		4		6
1		2	8		6	3	9	7
7			4		9	2		
	6			9			7	
			1				2	
4			2		3	9	5	
	5			1	2		3	
		3	9		7			1
		7	3	4	5	8		

6				1	9			
4	5			8				1
	8	1		7		6	3	
				3		7	5	
	6		2	4				3
		2			5	4	1	
2	1				8	3	7	
	7	8			4			9
	4	9		2	3	1		8

9 Light and Easy

		2	8	7	9		4	5
		7			4	9		
			2	6		8	7	
7	5						1	
9				5				7
3	8	6	7				5	
	6					1		2
	7	8	6			5	9	
	4	9	1	8	5			

4						1		6
8	3		1	7		5	9	
				4	6	3		
	1	7	4			6		5
3		8	7		1	2		
6			2	3				8
	2	4	3			8	6	
				4				
9		1		2		4	7	

		1	4			7		
9		8			6	1	4	
	7	2	1	3		8		
5		4	7		9		3	
				5		9		7
		7	3	8			1	
7		5	9				6	
	4			6				
8				4	3		7	9

9	3		2				8	6
	8					4	5	7
4	7			6		9		2
			4	7				3
						6		
5		9	1	8		2	7	4
1		7			4			9
					2			1
6				9		3		

	4	5	8	9				6
	2					9		
						7	2	5
5		7	9		6			2
	3			8				
	1		7	2		5		9
4			5	3				
	9	6	1					
3		1	2	6		8		

8	9							2
	7	4	1			8		
1			3		8	7		9
6				2				
				5			8	3
	8	2		3	9	6	7	
9	5							8
	1					9	3	
		3		8			2	

		9					2	3
5	6	8		7				
3		4	1			8		
			9			3		
8	7				1		5	
	9		4			6	1	
9			7		4			
	3		5	2	6			1
		2			3			

	3						4	5
				4				
			8	6		2		
						3		
9	2		7		6			8
3		4			9		2	6
2	4		6			5	3	
7		9			4	8		
			9	2			1	

17 Light and Easy

		6	5	8			2	
1	8			7				
5		9					1	6
7			6	4	3	5		
		5		1				
	4	1	7	2				
6	5	3						8
	1		4					
					8			7

9	3						4	
		8			9	1		2
2	6		5	1		3		
		3	2		5	6	1	7
							9	
1						2		
				4				
7			8	6	5			
	4	6			8			

19 Light and Easy

	6						1	2
		9	2			4	8	
			6		1	3		
5	3		4					7
	8				9	6		
	4			5	7	8	2	
4		3						
8	1	5	9		3			

8		3	7			1	6	
		7				4		
		5	1	9	8		2	
	5			4	9		3	
6				5		7		
	3						9	
							1	
		8						6
			8		5	9	7	

Light and Easy

		3		5			6	
8							3	
4			7		3	5		8
1				2	4	3		
3	6	4						
7				1				
				7				
			5		1		2	
5	7			6	9			

	9				5	2	1	7
6		1						5
			3					
					3	1	7	
			7			5		6
5	7		1		4	9		
		5						
				8				
	3	8		2	1		5	

Light and Easy

	1				7			
				6				3
		8		5		4	9	
	2	1	6	3			7	
						8		5
	3				5	6		
1				9	3		8	
		5	7			1	6	2

3		1	6			7		
4	2					1		
	6			5	2		9	
	8	3	5	1			4	
						3	6	
5			4	9				
				2				
7	4				5			9
					7			

25 Light and Easy

				9				
6				2	4		5	
							1	
4			8	5				1
	1	7						
					2	9	6	4
		4						5
	3	8	9	6		1		
				1	5		9	8

5	3			4	8		9	
7								
1			2					
	1				6			
4	9		8	3			1	2
2			4			7		3
	2					1		
6				9			8	
	4	1			2		3	6

	3	2						9
		8	2			4		
1		6	7		9			
	8		4			7		1
		7	1		3		9	2
			8		2			
		3						
6			9				5	
				8		9	2	6

			2					
		2		8	1	6	5	
	5			3			7	
3		4					6	
				4	3			2
5	2						4	
	4	5	8					3
1		9				4		
	8			6				1

29 Moderate

9						6		
7		1						9
	8			5				
	9		5		2		7	8
	6			1		9		
3	5	2		7	8			
		3			4			
	4		3			5		7
				9			1	

					6	8		
8	1		5				7	
4		7			8	6		2
3				4				8
2				3			4	
	8						9	1
							8	9
					5			
6			1	8		7	5	

31　Moderate

							9	
	5			9				4
4		2						
	1			6				
				3	4		7	
9		8	7				2	6
	3	1				5		7
7				5	6		8	
		9		4			6	

2		9						7
	1	6						
8				7				
				1	5	4		
	9	8			4	6		
				6		3	1	2
		1		4		2		
	3			2	6			
			3			1	9	

33 Moderate

	4	2			8			
				6			9	2
				7	3	5	4	
			7				5	1
	3				4			
4						8		
	5		8		7		3	4
6	9							
			6	5		2		

							4	5
	2	4			9		3	
1			3					9
		2						8
4			5					
3		7			6	9	5	
5	6		7			1	8	
	1	3						
7						3		

35 Moderate

	5							
	8				9	4		
	9					5		
9			1					5
	1	2		8			4	6
			2			7		
		1	7			2		
8				1				
	3		9		2	6		8

		4			5			
	8				3			
		5		2				9
			8			2		6
	7							1
2			1	7	6		5	
	1			3	7		9	
3								
		8	2	1				3

37 Moderate

		3			1	4		9
	8		6	3		7		
		1		6	3			8
	7	8			9			3
	4	2					1	
		9			6			
		4		5		3	9	7

					8	9		
		8		5			7	
			6	1				
	1				5	3		
2				9			1	
5	9		8	6				
	3					1		
	2	4					9	
			9	7		8		2

	3		4				6	
4							7	3
9		2		1				
8	7		9	2				1
		3		7		8		
				4			9	
					9			
	2	8						
				8	6		5	

1				8	5			7
				3				
	4					6	5	
5				7	6			
2	9							
		4	5		3		8	
	6					9	1	
			9					
3	7			2	4			

4				8			1	
			9			6	4	2
	9		7					
			8				7	3
	5			6				
						1	5	
2	8							
1				3	7		8	9
3		9						

5				4	2			9
9				3			2	
			7					
1			2			9		
	7				8		3	
		3	9					8
6		5				2	8	
		8				6	1	
			5					

43 Moderate

						1		
4			3	7				8
9								2
			6				3	
	8							
	9	7		1				4
2	7			6			5	
		6	1	5				
	5					3	2	

8	6	5						3
			4					6
					3	9		
5		2			9			
4		3			5	2		
				8				
6	7		1					
							1	
			2		4	7		9

45 Moderate

7	5			4				
	1		9	3				
	4	3			2			7
							4	3
1	7					9		
					1			6
5					4			
								1
9						6		5

8	2	9		7			3	
								1
						5		
	6	5		2	7			8
		1						3
				9		2		
7					4	9		
			6				5	
		6			2			

47 Moderate

8								6
6			2				8	
			5				1	
				7		5		8
		9						
		7		1		9		
	7		9					
5		1						4
		6	4	2		7		

		7						1
		9				6	5	
	2			7	9			3
	6					3		
9		4	5				6	
								8
		2	3			7	4	
8								
			6	9				

49 Moderate

			4				8	
1					2			
6		7						
	3	4						
5	6			1			2	
		9	6				7	
				5	3			9
							1	7
	2			4	9			

	6			4				
								6
		8						
	1			5			4	3
				8	3	7		5
						6		
	9						5	
	2		9		1	3		
4					6		1	

51 Demanding

					1			3
	1	4	9			8		
9			2					
8	6					5		7
4	9			2				
			3			9		
	2					3		
			6			1		
			7		8			2

			5	8				
9			6		7			
1	4							8
2			1					
					9		3	5
7		8						
		7		4		6		
						9		
			3		1	2	4	

53 Demanding

7			4					
	1	8						7
	9			1				
8		5		9		3		
		3	2			4		6
9		6						5
3								1
	8						2	
					7	5		

		2						
	9						4	
7	5				2	8	9	
5	2	1						8
				9				
3					5			
			6	3	7			4
		5		8				
	6		9			7		

55 Demanding

		2		4		1		
			7					
				6	8	7		4
5					7			6
							3	
	9			8		5		
2			6		3		1	
	4			1		9		
6					9			

		7		4				
			1					8
						3		
		9		2				
		1				6	8	5
		4	8			7		
3					7		5	
				8				4
1	7				5	8		9

57 Demanding

7			4	3			8	
						9	5	
1								
		1	6					
	4	9				7	6	
2					4			3
			5		7			
				1	3		7	
5		4		2				

		4		7			5	9
		9		2	6			
3	6		4					8
	3		2		8			
	4	1					3	
								6
						7	1	
	5			3				2
		8						

59   Demanding

		2		6				
6		8			7			
	1	7		3				5
		5		4			8	
					2			9
				5			3	6
			9					2
	8	6	3	1	4			
4								

3								8
	5				4		6	
				5	7			
				7				6
		4						
9		4			6		5	7
1	3					2		
					9			
7	2				8	9		

61 Demanding

		9	4		7			
2		7	5			4		
	5			8				6
3					6			8
	7					2		
	9		7	1	3			
					5		3	
	6		9					5
						1		

		3			2			
4	7				9	5		
		5	8					
		6			1		2	
		7		5		3	4	
2			4		3			
							1	
				8				2
			1		7		9	

63 Demanding

7			3	8				
1			5					
6		2						
5		4		6		2		
		3				4		1
							8	9
	5					3		
	7			3			1	4
			7		8			

	7		9			6		
			1		2	7		
5	4						1	
4		7	2				9	8
								7
				3	4			
7						1		
6						2		
	3	2	8		5			

65 Demanding

6			1					4
						2		
	2	8			7			9
						8		1
7	1	2		5				
	9						6	
		4				1		8
				1	9			
			8		3			

7	6	9			2	8		
		5		3				
			1			2	6	
		3	9					
				8			9	5
	8	2						1
			8		4	7		
		6						3

67 Demanding

							8	
8			1		4		5	
		5						
1	8			4				
		9			3		1	8
	6		5				7	
	4	7		6		2		
					9	7		
	2							9

Demanding **68**

			7			2		6
		8						
		7	9	5				1
5	7			1			9	
					2			
						3	4	
	3		8					
				6			1	
4						6		9

69   Demanding

2								
				5	6		8	
								7
				6	3	5		
9	1	7				8		
		4	1			2		
							9	
5		8	9	2		7		

	3					2		
			4	7				
5			6			8		
				9				
9		6						3
3		8			1		2	
	1				2			4
					5		7	
	7						9	

				4				
7		9			8			
5							2	
	3		9	7				
2					5			4
								9
	1			6		8		
	4						3	
9				5	4	6		

				1	6			9
	8							
3					5	2		
		3					7	
		2					4	6
			7					1
7		9			1			
	2			5				8
6					4			2

73 Demanding

		7				4	5	
8					4			
			2		7			
	6	9	4					8
2		8					1	9
					3			
	2	4						6
	9	3				8		
				6				

					2	1		7
	1			6				4
	5				7			6
	6	7		4				
				3			9	2
5								
2	3				8		5	
4								
				5				

75 Demanding

9	4							8
2					1			
7	1				5		2	
							7	
		7	2	3				
			4				5	
		6				8		3
	2		5		9		1	

		7	6					1
		1				3		2
3	9		1					
8		3			9			
6		2			1		3	
			2			6		
	8					7		
			4	7				
	3	9				8		

					9	8	4	2
	9		1					
4		8						7
5		4					6	
6								5
	8				7			
	1	6				9		
					2	3	8	
			8		1			

8					5			
								3
		9		6			7	5
6	3		7		4		9	
4	2			9	1			
								8
2		5						
					7	3	6	
	6			4		1		

79 Beware! Very Challenging!

			3			5	6	
	9	1						
		8					4	
			8		7			3
		9	5			2	8	
	4							5
							9	6
5					8			2
		4			1			

80

					5			
2	8			7			6	
	6	7				1		3
6	5					9		
		9	5		1			
					7		8	
	3							
1					2		5	
	9				3		7	

81 Beware! Very Challenging!

					3		9	
	2		8	9	1		3	
		7				6		
1								
6	4							
8		2	6		7	4	1	
			2	3				
						8	7	
		8	1					

9			4				7	
	7	1						8
					6		1	
				5		8	6	
		2	9	1				
	3					7	2	
						3		5
4				6				
		3						

83 Beware! Very Challenging!

	3	1	9	8				7
							1	
	6			7	1	3		
	8	9					2	4
			7			8		
5							3	
6	1							8
		8	3		9	2		5

9								
		8				7		3
				9	4		5	
	1				6	2	3	4
		3		4		9		
		7		2				
	7	1						
					9	8	2	
			7					

85 Beware! Very Challenging!

	8		6			1		
								8
					3		5	
2		8		6				9
	7							
	1				5	3	6	
4	6			5	7		8	
								1
			1			9		

					2		9	
		5		1	4	7		
	7							8
	4	3				5		
			4					
			7	6	8	3		
	1					9	2	3
				9				
8					5			1

87 Beware! Very Challenging!

				7	9			1
			6	1			7	
7						4		8
			9	2		3	8	
	9		5		7			
	1			8				6
4							5	
	2	5	4				3	

	5	4		2			6	
2	1							
3					8	5		
5		9		7				
			9				2	
4					6			
		3						4
		6	8			9		7

89 Beware! Very Challenging!

3	9						8	
6				1			5	2
	4							3
		4						
					3	8		6
			2		6			5
	5							
	1				9	6		4
				7				1

		1						
3	5							
9		4	7			5	2	
4	1			2			7	
	6		8			9		
	2	8						
		5	1		9	7		
					6			9
			3		8			

91 Beware! Very Challenging!

		1	3	2				
7		6			1			5
		2	4					1
9								2
						3		
8	1	7						
		5			9	6		
					6			3
				5	2			8

Beware! Very Challenging!

92

					7	9		
3	2							
8			4			2		
6			8			4		
9		5	7		2	6		
7			5				9	
		4			6			
5						7	6	
	3				5			

93 Beware! Very Challenging!

8								
	9	6						7
7						5	6	
		5	3	8			9	
		3		7				8
4							2	
1		2			3			
	5		8	6				4
				1			7	

				9				
4		7				5		
	2				1			4
8	5					9		
			3			6	1	
2					4			
6							8	7
	7	1	6					
				2			3	

Beware! Very Challenging!

7			6					
	8					5	4	
			8		3	2		7
					1		2	
						1		
9		5	3			4		
	9				4		6	
				7	6	3		
	5							2

	4	7			2		1	
5						8		
				9		7		
6			2					4
	3		1	4				
	9			3				6
			3				8	
1	2		8	7		3		

Beware! Very Challenging!

		9		8		4		3
1				5				
3	4					5		
	3	4	1		6	2		
	1				5	6		
	6	7		9		3		5
	2					1		
				4	2			
			7					

						3		
9				1				5
6	8				9			
		6			8		9	
1			4					
8	3					7		
	9		5		4		1	
	7		2	3				
							2	

99   Beware! Very Challenging!

			2	4				
	8	1	5	7			6	
	6				8	9	7	
		6				7	8	1
								9
	2	9			1		3	6
	3	2	4			1	9	8
			8					
	7			9				2

	2	6			5		4	3
4						9		
	3		7				8	
	5			6	8	1		
	4				7			
				1				2
		1						5
7			9					

	1	2	3	4	5	6	7	8	9
a	8	1	7	4	6	3	9	2	5
b	2	5	4	1	9	7	3	8	6
c	9	3	6	8	2	5	1	4	7
d	6	7	9	5	8	4	2	1	3
e	1	4	8	3	7	2	5	6	9
f	5	2	3	6	1	9	4	7	8
g	3	8	5	2	4	6	7	9	1
h	4	9	1	7	3	8	6	5	2
i	7	6	2	9	5	1	8	3	4

Step-by-step Solving Guide 1

Let's start in the middle box, which already contains six numbers. Still miss-ing there are the 1, 2, and 9. Both 2 and 9 already appear in column *5*, so the only number left for square *f5* is 1. So you can fill in the 1 there. How about the 2 and 9? There is already a 9 in row *e*. So the 9 in the middle box has to go in row *f*—in square *f6*. The 2 must go in the only remaining empty square, *e6*. This completes the middle box.

In row *i*, 1 and 4 are missing. Square *i6* has to contain the 1, as there is already a 4 in column *6*. Therefore, the 4 goes in square *i9*. The remaining numbers in column *9* are 1, 2, and 6. As the lower-right box already con-tains a 6, the 6 in this column must go in *b9*. The 1 goes in *g9*, because this row already contains a 2. This leaves us the 2 for *h9*.

The upper-left box is a good place to continue now. Because you already entered a 6 in row *b*, the two remaining numbers of this row must be 2 and 4. Column *1* already has a 4, so square *b1* must get the 2, and by elimina-tion square *b3* gets the 4. The remaining numbers for the upper-left box are

1, 6, and 8. Columns *2* and *3* already have 8's, so the 8 goes in *a1*. And column *2* already has a 6, so the 6 goes in *c3*. This leaves the 1 for *a2*.

Row *c* lacks just 4, 5, and 8. Because the upper-right box already has a 5 and 8, the 4 must go in *c8*. This leaves the 8 for square *c4* (there is already a 5 in this column) and the 5 for *c6*. Which completes row *c*.

In column *4* the only remaining number is 4, so fill it in. And in the upper-right box, the only remaining number is 2. The two remaining numbers in row *a* are 3 and 6. The 6 has to go in *a5*, because column *6* already contains a 6, which leaves the 3 for *a6*.

Column *6* now has only one empty square (*b6*), so we might as well put an 8 in it. The lower-middle box has two empty squares remaining. Put a 4 in *g5*, because row *h* already has a 4. By elimination, *h5* gets the 3. The remaining squares in row *h* have to contain, from left to right: 9 (since 1 and 5 already appear in column *2*), 1 (since 5 already appears in this box), and 5. Now 3's are the only remaining numbers for the lower-left box (square *g1*) and column *3* (*f3*).

The remaining numbers in columns *1, 2, 7,* and *8* can be entered right away. Column *1,* top to bottom: 6 (1 and 5 already in row *d*), 1 (1 already in row *f*), and 5. Column *2,* top to bottom: 7 (only remaining number in this row), 4 (2 already in row *e*), and 2. Column *7,* top to bottom: 5 (4 and 7 already in this row), 4 (4 already in row *g*), and 7. Column *8,* top to bottom: 6, 7, and 9, in all cases, because these are the only remaining numbers in their rows. In fact, the only remaining numbers of this first sudoku!

	1	2	3	4	5	6	7	8	9
a	1	6	9	7	5	2	3	8	4
b	3	2	4	8	1	6	5	7	9
c	7	5	8	3	4	9	1	2	6
d	8	4	6	5	9	3	7	1	2
e	9	1	2	4	8	7	6	3	5
f	5	3	7	2	6	1	9	4	8
g	4	8	1	9	3	5	2	6	7
h	6	7	5	1	2	4	8	9	3
i	2	9	3	6	7	8	4	5	1

Step-by-step Solving Guide 2

Let's start with the upper-left box. Because there's already a 7 in row *a*, the 7 has to go in *c1*. Now only 6 and 9 must be placed. There is already a 6 in column *3*, so *a2* must get the 6 and *a3* the 9. Moving to the right, to the upper-middle box, a 3 has to go in *c4*, the only possible square for a 3 in that row, as there are already 3's in columns *8* and *9*. As there is already a 6 in row *a*, the only possibility left for a 6 in this box is *b6*. Let's look for a moment at square *g6*. A 5 has to go in *g6*, as all the other numbers are in its row, column, or box. How do we know that? Row *g* has 1, 3, 2; column *6* has 6, 9, 1, 4, 8; the center box has 1, 2, 8. The only number missing when looking at these groups all together is 5. So *g6* must have a 5. This means the 5 cannot go in *a6* and has to go to *a5*—which leaves the 2 for *a6*.

　　Two boxes at the top are completed, so let's fill the third box at the top-right. Being the last square in its row, *a7* has to have a 3, and *b9* a 9. The 2 for column *8* cannot go in either of the two boxes below it because there's already a 2 in the lower-right box, and because there's already a 2 in row *f*.

So the only remaining square for the 2 in column *8* is *c8*. Which leaves *c9* for the 6. One third done!

Let's switch to columns. Remaining in column *5* are 2, 6, and 9. Square *d5* has to contain a 9, because of the 6 in this row and the 2 in this box. This same 2 makes the 6 go to *f5*, which leaves the 2 for *h5*. In column *6*, the numbers 3 and 7 are remaining. Because of the 7 in row *d* and the 3 in row *e*, *d6* gets the 3, and *e6* the 7. Remaining in column *7* are 8 and 9. There is already an 8 in row *f*, so we can enter an 8 in *h7* and a 9 in *f7*.

We've completed three boxes and three columns, we might as well do three rows now: *d, e,* and *f*. In row *d*, square *d1* has to contain an 8, because the middle and the middle-right boxes already have 8's. The middle box has a 2 already, so this number must be entered in *d9*, leaving *d4* for the 5. The remaining 7 of row *f* goes to *f3*, as no other number can be entered there, and the 4 goes to *f8*.

The remaining numbers in row *e* are 1, 2, 4, 5, and 9. Square *e4* has to contain a 4, and *e9* a 5, as both numbers are the only missing numbers in their respective boxes. As the lower-left box already has a 1, *e2* is the only option for a 1 in this column. Which leaves us *e1* for the 9 (there is a 9 already in column *3*), and *e3* for the 2.

Just the three bottom rows left. As for row *h*, you can enter 6 in *h1*, because it's the only number missing from both row *h* and column *1*. Using the same reasoning, 5 goes in *h3*, and 9 in *h8*. This same logic applies for row *g*: enter 4 in *g1*, 6 in *g8*, 9 in *g4*, 8 in *g2*, and 7 in *g9*. The remaining squares are all the last remaining squares in each column: 2 in *i1*, 9 in *i2*, 3 in *i3*, 6 in *i4*, 5 in *i8*, and 1 in *i9*.

	1	2	3	4	5	6	7	8	9
a	5	3	2	1	4	8	6	9	7
b	7	8	4	9	6	5	3	2	1
c	1	6	9	2	7	3	4	5	8
d	3	1	7	5	2	6	8	4	9
e	4	9	6	8	3	7	5	1	2
f	2	5	8	4	1	9	7	6	3
g	9	2	3	6	8	4	1	7	5
h	6	7	5	3	9	1	2	8	4
i	8	4	1	7	5	2	9	3	6

Step-by-step Solving Guide 26

Why is this puzzle more difficult than the previous ones? Although deciding on difficulty can be subjective, there is one clear-cut criterion. In all previous puzzles, when going from one empty square to another, there would always be one square where only one number would be possible, as the other numbers from 1–9 would already be present in the same row, column, or box.

Here, this is not the case. In each square, there are at least two numbers still possible. Therefore, we need to find another way to solve. The other way is not going by the square, but going by the number: please have a look at column 2. It still has four empty squares, and for each square there are at least two numbers possible. But what if we check this column, going by the numbers, for instance, number 7?

A 7 is no longer possible in *b2* and *c2*, because of the 7 in this box. A 7 is also no longer possible in *f2*, because of the 7 in row *f*. Therefore, *h2* is the only remaining possibility for a 7 in column 2. After this, the same applies to the 5: because of the 5 in the upper-left box, the only place for it in column 2 is *f2*.

After this 5 in *f2*, row *f* can be completed: put a 1 in *f5* (all other numbers are in this row, column, or box), and for the same reason a 9 in *f6*, a 6 in *f8*, and an 8 in *f3*. Moving one row up, we can apply the same logic for *e7*, which has to contain a 5 because the other numbers are already in this row or box. As a result, *e3* can only contain a 6 for the same reason, leaving *e6* for the 7.

Of the remaining 3 and 7 in the middle-left box, the 7 has to go to *d3*, as column *1* already has a 7. Therefore, *d1* has to get the 3. Same for the middle box where 2 and 5 are remaining: as column *4* has a 2 already, the 2 has to go to *d5*, leaving *d4* for the 5.

The only possible number left for *i7* is a 9, as the other numbers are already in this row, column, or box. So we now have a 9 in column *7*. There is also a 9 in column *8*, which leaves the 9 in column *9*. As the upper- and lower-right boxes already have one, this 9 has to go in the middle-right box, where *d9* is the only possible square in this column. The remaining 8 in this box has to be in *d7*, as there is already an 8 in column *8*, leaving *d8* for the 4.

Square *i5* is the only possible place for a 5 in row *i*, because of the 5's in columns *1* and *4*. This results in *g5* being the only possible square in column *5* for the 8, because of the 8 in the upper-middle box. The remaining 7 in column *5* has to go to *c5*, as there is already a 7 in row *b*, leaving *b5* for the 6.

The 9 in column *1* can only go to *g1*, because of the 9 in row *i*. Square *i1* therefore has to contain the 8. The 6 in column *2* has to go to *c2*, because of the 6 in row *2*, leaving *b2* for the 8.

Row *a* still needs a 1, 2, 6, and 7. Square *a3* gets the 2, as 1, 6, and 7 are already in the upper-left box. This leaves 6 for *a7*, as 1 and 7 are already in column *7*. The upper-middle box has a 7 already, so the 1 goes to *a4*, and the 7 to *a9*.

Let's do the rest columnwise. Column *4* has 3, 6, 7, and 9 still missing. The 9 has to go to *b4* (already a 9 in the lower-middle box), the 7 to *i4* (last number in this row), the 6 to *g4* (6 already in row *h*), and the 3 to *h4*.

Remaining in column *8* are 2, 5, and 7. The 7 has to go to *g8* (there is a 7 in the upper-right box), the 2 to *b8* (there is a 2 in row *c*), and the 5 to *c8*. In column *6* we still need 1, 3, 4, and 5. The 1 can only to go *h6* (1's in row *g* and in the upper-middle box), the 4 to *g6* (a 4 in the upper-middle box), a 5 to *b6* (a 5 in row *c*), and a 3 to *c6*.

When looked at in the right order, the remaining squares can all be filled because there is just one number possible (all the other numbers are already in its row, column, or box): a 4 in *b3*, a 9 in *c3*, a 3 in *b7*, a 1 in *b9*, a 4 in *c7*, an 8 in *c9*, a 5 in *h3*, a 3 in *g3*, a 2 in *h7*, a 5 in *g9*, and a 4 in *h9*.

	1	2	3	4	5	6	7	8	9
a	7	3	2	5	4	8	6	1	9
b	9	5	8	2	6	1	4	7	3
c	1	4	6	7	3	9	2	8	5
d	2	8	5	4	9	6	7	3	1
e	4	6	7	1	5	3	8	9	2
f	3	1	9	8	7	2	5	6	4
g	8	9	3	6	2	5	1	4	7
h	6	2	4	9	1	7	3	5	8
i	5	7	1	3	8	4	9	2	6

Step-by-step Solving Guide 27

In column *1*, the 8 can only go to *g1*, as there are 8's in the upper- and middle-left boxes, and in row *i*. The 2 can only go to *d1*, because of the 2's in the upper-left box and in rows *e*, *f*, and *i*. Still in column *1*, the 3 has to go in *f1*, because of the 3's in the upper- and lower-left boxes and in row *e*. And the 9 has to go in *b1*, because of the 9's in rows *a*, *e*, and *i*.

Looking at column *7*, the only number possible in *g7* is a 1, as all the other numbers are present in this row, column, or box. (That is, for *g7*, its box has 5, 9, 2, 6; its column has 4, 7, 9; its row has 8, 3. The only number missing in these three groups together is 1.) Square *c7* has to contain a 2 (there are 2's already in row *a* and in both boxes below the upper one), and a 3 must go to *h7* (3's already in rows *a*, *e*, and *f*).

The 8 in column *6* can only go to *a6*, because of the 8 in row *b* and 8's in both boxes below the upper one. Because of this, the 8 in column *7* has to go to *e7*, as there are now 8's in rows *a* and *f*. Continuing with the 8's: the one in the lower-right box has to be in *h9*, as there is one already in row *g*.

Only one 8 missing now: it has to be in the upper-right box in *c8*, as all the other rows and columns have one.

In the middle box, the 7 has to be in *f5*, because of the 7's in rows *d* and *e*. In column *5*, the 9 has to be in *d5*, as there are 9's in the upper-middle and lower-middle boxes and in row *e*.

In row *d*, square *d3* can only contain a 5, because all other numbers are already in this row, column, or box (see the explanation of this above), and *d6* therefore gets a 6. By elimination too, *e1* can only have a 4, *e2* a 6, *e5* a 5, and *d8* a 3. In column *3*, the 9 has to go to *f3*, because of the 9's in rows *h* and *i*. Leaving as the only square in the middle-left box *f2*, a nice place for the 1.

In column *2*, the 9 has to go to *g2*, as there are 9's in the upper-left box and in rows *h* and *i*. Which leaves *h2* in this column for a 2, as there is a 2 in the upper-left box and in row *i*. The 2 in the lower-middle box now has to be in *g5*, as all the other rows and columns have 2's.

In row *a*, the 4 can only be in *a5*, as the columns *1* and *4* and the upper-right box have 4's. This enables us to complete column *5*: a 6 can only go to *b5* (6's in rows *c* and *h*), a 3 to *c5* (3 in row *h*), and a 1 to *h5*.

If we work in the right order, the rest can all be done by elimination. In each case, just one number is possible for a particular square because the other numbers are already in its row, column, and box. So you can enter: a 5 in *c9*, a 4 in *f9*, a 7 in *g9*, a 3 in *b9*, which completes column *9*.

In the same fashion, by elimination, enter a 4 in *h3*, a 1 in *i3*, a 7 in *h6*, a 5 in *a4*, a 1 in *b6*, a 3 in *i4*, a 6 in *g4*, a 4 in *g8*, a 5 in *g6*, and a 4 in *i6*, which completes columns *3*, *4*, *5*, and *6*.

Continuing by elimination, *f7* can only contain a 5, *f8* a 6, *a7* a 6, *a8* a 1, *b8* a 7, *b2* a 5, *a1* a 7, *c2* a 4, *i1* a 5, and finally, *i2* a 7.

	1	2	3	4	5	6	7	8	9
a	5	8	7	4	6	1	2	9	3
b	2	1	4	9	7	3	8	5	6
c	9	3	6	2	8	5	7	1	4
d	8	6	3	1	4	9	5	2	7
e	4	9	5	8	2	7	6	3	1
f	1	7	2	3	5	6	9	4	8
g	6	2	8	5	1	4	3	7	9
h	7	4	9	6	3	2	1	8	5
i	3	5	1	7	9	8	4	6	2

Step-by-step Solving Guide 51

The start of this sudoku is not particularly demanding: by elimination (that is, no other number will fit because they are already in that row, column, or box), *e7* must get a 6, *i7* a 4, *c7* a 7, and *a7* a 2, which completes column *7*. In the upper-right box, a 9 has to go to *a8*, because of the 9's in rows *b* and *c*. And in the upper-left box, you can enter a 2 in *b1*, as rows *a* and *c* have a 2 already.

Before it becomes really demanding, we can enter two more numbers. In column *2*, the 4 has to go to *h2*, because of the 4's in the upper-left and middle-left boxes and in row *i*. And in column *6*, the only possible place for a 2 is *h6*, because of the 2's in the upper-middle and middle boxes and the 2 in row *g*.

But now what? In each square at least two numbers are possible. And in each row, column, or box there are at least two possible locations for each number. So how to proceed? The answer is a technique needed for all demanding puzzles, which will be described next.

In column *1*, a 3 is not possible in *a1*, because of the 3 in row *a*. Same with *f1* (a 3 is in row *f*) and *g1* (a 3 is in row *g*). So the 3 in column *1* must be in either *h1* or *i1*. Both these squares are in the lower-left box. This means that although we do not yet know where the 3 has to be in that box, it will go to either *h1* or *i1*, and *certainly not* to any of the other squares in that box!

Now have a look at *i2:* this column contains 1, 2, 4, 6, and 9, and this row 2, 4, 7, and 8. Plain elimination would leave both 3 and 5 as possibilities for *i2*. But now we know that a 3 will go to another square in this box (*h1* or *i1*), which rules out a 3 as a possibility for *i2*. So we can enter a 5 in *i2!*

This was the small push needed in order to continue: by elimination, *f2* can now only contain a 7, *a2* an 8, *c2* a 3, *i8* a 6, *b8* a 5, and *b9* a 6. The only place for an 8 in column *4* is *e4*, as there are 8's in rows *a* and *d*, and in the lower-middle box. As a result, row *e* can be completed by elimination: *e9* can only get a 1, *e8* a 3, *e3* a 5, and *e6* a 7.

In the upper-left box, the 5 has to be in *a1*, as there is a 5 in column *3*. The 7 goes to *a3* (a 7 is in row *c*) and *c3* gets the 6. In the upper-right box, *c8* can only contain a 1, and *c9* a 4. In the upper-middle box, by elimination, *a4* can only have a 4, *a5* a 6, *b5* a 7, *b6* a 3, *c6* a 5, and *c5* an 8.

In row *d*, the 3 has to go to *d3* (3's are in the middle and middle-right boxes), and 2 to *d8* (a 2 is in the middle box). In row *f*, by elimination, *f1* can only contain a 1, *f3* a 2, *f9* an 8, *f8* a 4, *f5* a 5, and *f6* a 6.

The rest follows by elimination: *g1* a 6, *h1* a 7, *i1* a 3 (at last!), *g4* a 5, *d4* a 1, *g8* a 7, *h8* an 8, *h9* a 5, *g9* a 9, *g3* an 8, *i3* a 1, *h3* a 9, *h5* a 3, *i5* a 9, *g6* a 4, *d6* a 9, *d5* a 4, and finally, *g5* a 1.

	1	2	3	4	5	6	7	8	9
a	6	7	2	5	8	4	3	1	9
b	9	8	3	6	1	7	5	2	4
c	1	4	5	2	9	3	7	6	8
d	2	5	9	1	3	8	4	7	6
e	4	6	1	7	2	9	8	3	5
f	7	3	8	4	6	5	1	9	2
g	5	1	7	9	4	2	6	8	3
h	3	2	4	8	7	6	9	5	1
i	8	9	6	3	5	1	2	4	7

Step-by-step Solving Guide 52

By elimination, *i9* has to get a 7. In column *2*, the 7 can only be in *a2*, as there are 7's in row *b* and in the middle-left and lower-left boxes. In row *b*, *b2* is the only possibility for an 8, because of the 8's in column *3* and in the upper-middle and upper-right boxes. Square *b5* has to contain a 1, being the only place for a 1 in column *5* (1's are in row *c* and in the middle and lower-middle boxes).

In the upper-middle box, the only remaining place for a 4 is *a6*, as row *c* has a 4 already. The 8 in row *i* can only be in *i1*, because of the 8's in columns *2*, *3*, and *5*. Which concludes the straightforward solving before the demanding part starts.

In row *e*, a 2 can only be in either *e4* or *e5*, as there are already 2's in the middle-left box and in column *7*. Both *e4* and *e5* are in the middle box, so the 2 of this box will be either in *e4* or *e5*, and not in any of the other squares in the middle box.

Now have a look at *f4*: row *f* has a 7 and an 8, column *4* has 1, 3, 5, and

6, and the middle box 1 and 9. So this leaves 2 and 4 as possibilities for *f4*. But the 2 of this box has to go to *e4* or *e5*, which means 4 is the only number left for *f4!*

By elimination, *f7* now has to get a 1, *a7* a 3, *a1* a 6, *a3* a 2, and *e1* a 4. In the upper-left box, *b3* gets the 3, as this is the only place in this row for a 3 (there is a 3 in the upper-right box). Which leaves *c3* for the 5. Column *7* can be completed by elimination: *c7* has to have a 7, *e7* an 8, *d7* a 4, and *b7* a 5. In row *b*, *b8* can only contain a 2, and *b9* a 4.

The 5 in column *1* is in either *g1* or *h1*, both of which are in the lower-left square. So neither *i2* nor *i3* can contain a 5, which leaves *i5* as the only possible square for a 5 in row *i*. As a result, in column *5*, *c5* is the only place for the 9, because of 9's in the middle box and in row *h*.

In row *c*, a 6 goes to *c8* (a 6 is in the upper-middle box), a 3 to *c6* (a 3 is in column *4*), and a 2 in *c4*. This now eliminates the possibility of a 2 at *e4*, so the 2 must go in *e5*. In column *4*, *g4* can only house a 9, *h4* an 8, and *e4* a 7. In column *6*, by elimination, *g6* can only have a 2, *h6* a 6 (completing the lower-middle box as we go by entering a 7 in *h5*), *f6* a 5, and *d6* an 8.

The rest can be done by elimination: *f8* can only have a 9, *d9* a 6, *f9* a 2, *d8* a 7, *a8* a 1, *a9* a 9, *d3* a 9, *d5* a 3, *d2* a 5, *f5* a 6, *f2* a 3, *h8* a 5, *g8* an 8, *h1* a 3, *g1* a 5, *g2* a 1, *h2* a 2, *i3* a 6, *i2* a 9, *h3* a 4, *e3* a 1, *e2* a 6, *g9* a 3, and finally, *h9* a 1.

	1	2	3	4	5	6	7	8	9
a	4	2	7	6	3	5	9	8	1
b	5	6	1	9	8	7	3	4	2
c	3	9	8	1	2	4	5	6	7
d	8	4	3	7	6	9	2	1	5
e	6	7	2	8	5	1	4	3	9
f	9	1	5	2	4	3	6	7	8
g	1	8	4	3	9	2	7	5	6
h	2	5	6	4	7	8	1	9	3
i	7	3	9	5	1	6	8	2	4

Step-by-step Solving Guide 76

Before coming to the really challenging clues, we will first deal with some columns. To start, column *4* can be done quickly by elimination (again, "by elimination" means that only a single number is missing when you consider all the numbers already accounted for in a square's row, column, and box): *i4* can only contain a 5, *d4* a 7, *e4* an 8, *b4* a 9, and *g4* a 3. In column *3*, the 8 can only go to *c3*, as there are 8's in the middle-left and lower-left boxes.

In column *1*, the only place for the 9 is *f1*, as there are 9's in both the upper-left and lower-left boxes. Square *i1* gets a 7, because of a 7 in the upper-left box and in rows *g* and *h*.

In column *5*, a 9 goes to *g5* (9's are in the upper-middle and middle boxes and in row *i*), a 1 goes to *i5* (1's are in the upper-middle and middle boxes), and a 6 goes to *d5*, as there are 6's in the upper-middle box and in rows *e* and *f*.

In column *9*, an 8 goes to *f9* (8's are in rows *c, d,* and *e,* and in the lower-right box), a 3 goes to *h9* (3's are in rows *c, d, e, g,* and *i*), a 9 goes to *e9* (9's are in rows *c*, *d*, *g*, and *i*), and a 7 goes to *c9* (7's are in row *d* and in the lower-right box).

Now it gets more demanding. In column *5*, a 2 goes to either *a5* or *c5*, as there are 2's in row *2* and in the middle box. These two squares are all in the upper-middle box, which means that 2's cannot go to any of the other squares in this box. Now have a look at row *c*: a 2 is not possible in *c7* nor in *c8*, because of the 2 in the upper-right box. We now know a 2 is also not possible in *c6*, which leaves *c5* for the 2!

Three 7's are remaining: the one in the upper-middle box goes to *b6* (7's are in rows *a* and *c* and in column *5*), the one in the middle-right box goes to *f8* (7's are in row *d* and in column *7*), and the one in the middle-left box goes to *e2* (7's are in rows *d* and *f*).

We can find three 6's as well: in the upper-left box in *b2* (a 6 is in row *a* and in column *1*), in the upper-right box in *c8* (6's are in rows *a* and *b* and in column *7*), and in the lower-left box in *h3* (6's are in columns *1, 2, 7,* and *8*, and in *h6* goes an 8, because of the 8's in rows *g* and *i*). And the only place in row *f* for a 1 is *f2*, because of the 1's in column 3 and in the middle box.

Now it gets really interesting. Studying column *7*, it turns out that both 1 and 2 can only appear in either *d7* or *h7*: both numbers are in the upper-right box and both are in row *e*. This means that any other number cannot go there: because if, for instance, we would enter a 9 in *h7*, both 1 and 2 would have to go to *d7*. As there cannot be two numbers in one square, *d7* and *h7* need to remain restricted for the 1 and the 2 in any order.

This means that a 9 has to go in *a7*: it cannot go in *c7*, *d7*, nor *e7* (9's are in those rows), and also not in *h7*, as explained above, which leaves only *a7*. As a result, a 9 goes to *h8*: there are 9's in rows *g* and *i* and in column *7*.

As explained earlier, *h7* houses a 1 or a 2. Therefore, the 5 in that row is in *h1* or *h2*. Both are in the same box, so a 5 cannot go to any of the other squares in this box. Knowing this, a 4 can be entered in *g3*, the only possible number in this square. Leaving in column *3*, *f3* for a 5, leaving in the middle-left box *d2* for a 4.

The rest is simple elimination, no need to explain the details to an expert! In each case, just one number is possible in each square because the other numbers are already in its row, column, or box: *d9* can only get a 5, *g9* a 6, *i9* a 4, *i8* a 2, *g6* a 2, *i6* a 6, *e7* a 4, *e5* a 5, *c7* a 5, *h7* a 1, *d7* a 2, *d8* a 1, *c6* a 4, *g8* a 5, *g1* a 1, *f6* a 3, *f5* a 4, *a6* a 5, *b5* an 8, *a5* a 3, *b8* a 4, *a8* an 8, *b1* a 5, *a2* a 2, *a1* a 4, *h1* a 2, and *h2* a 5.

	1	2	3	4	5	6	7	8	9
a	1	2	6	8	9	5	7	4	3
b	4	7	8	6	2	3	9	5	1
c	5	3	9	7	4	1	2	8	6
d	6	1	7	2	5	9	4	3	8
e	9	5	3	4	6	8	1	2	7
f	8	4	2	1	3	7	5	6	9
g	3	9	4	5	1	6	8	7	2
h	2	8	1	3	7	4	6	9	5
i	7	6	5	9	8	2	3	1	4

Step-by-step Solving Guide 100

As a warm-up, 7's go to *a7* (no other number is possible there), *h5* (7's are in row *i* and in columns *4* and *6*), and to *g8* (7's are in rows *h* and *i* and in column *7*). The only place for a 9 in the lower-right box is *h8* (9's are in row *i* and in column *7*). And now over to the real stuff!

In column *2*, because the lower-left box already has both a 1 and 7, these two numbers can only go to either *b2* or *d2*. These two squares must be reserved for these two numbers, and so cannot have any other number. This means the only place left for a 9 in this column is *g2*, as there are 9's already in rows *h* and *i*.

Next, we have a variation of the previous theme. In column *9*, there are again two numbers that play the lead role: this time 1 and 6. These two numbers can still go to more than two squares, so this is different than before, but the point is that there are exactly two squares where these two numbers are the only possible candidates: *b9* and *c9*.

This means that any of these two numbers 1 and 6 cannot go to another square in this column. Because if a 1 would go to *h9*, for instance, the only possible candidate for both *b9* and *c9* would be one single number, a 6!

Keeping this in mind, we know now that in row *i* a 1 has to go to *i8*, as there are 1's in the lower-left and lower-middle boxes and in column *7*, and we cannot put a 1 in *h9*!

And now the pièce de résistance! First there is what is called an X-wing: in row *a*, a 1 can only be in *a1* or in *a4* (a 1 is in column *5*). In row *f*, a 1 can only be in *f1* or *f4* (1's are in columns *3* and *5* and in the middle-right box). If you mark these squares and connect *a1* with *f4*, and *f1* with *a4*, you get an X.

Should *a1* get a 1, *f1* cannot get one anymore, which means *f4* will, as *f1* and *f4* are the only options for a 1 in row *f*. Should *a1* *not* get a 1, *a4* will, so *f4* can no longer get a 1, which means *f1* will get a 1. Therefore, either both *a1* and *f4* have a 1, or both *f1* and *a4* have a 1.

In column *1*, therefore, there is a 1 in either *a1* or *f1*, which means there cannot be a 1 in any of the other squares in this column. (The same applies to column *4*, and *a4* and *f4*.) This means that, by elimination, *c1* can only have a 5 or 9, *e1* a 2, 3, or 9, *g1* a 3 or 5 (remember: the 6 and 8 in this box are in *h2* and *i2*, because in column *2*, 1 and 7 are in *b2* and *d2*, see above!), and *h1* a 2 or 3.

As a result, squares *c1*, *e1*, *g1*, and *h1* contain the numbers 2, 3, 5, and 9 in any order. So four different numbers for four different squares. This means that none of these four numbers can be in any of the other squares in this column, the same principle as before with the 1 and 6 in column *9*!

Therefore, *a1* cannot get a 9, and because of the 9 in column *4*, the only place left for a 9 in row *a* is *a5*! So, at last, you can actually put in a real number there! You will probably understand by now why this is puzzle #100.

In column *6*, the only place for a 9 is *d6*, as 9's are already in the upper-middle and lower-middle boxes. The only place for a 1 in row *d* is *d2*, as *d1* and *d4* cannot have a 1 (remember the X-wing!), and as there are 1's in columns *3* and *5* and in the middle-right box.

This leaves for column *2* a 7 in *b2* (a 7 is in the lower-left box). The only place for a 1 in the upper-left box is now *a1*, as *c1* cannot have a 1 (X-wing!), and there is a 1 in column *3*. And as *a1* has a 1 now, *f4* must have one too (X-wing!).

That is all the fireworks, we will do the rest quickly. Row *a* has only one square left: so an 8 goes to *a4*. As a result, the only place for an 8 in column *5* is *i5* (8's are in the upper-middle and middle boxes).

If done in the right order, the rest is a matter of elimination: *i2* can only contain a 6, *h2* an 8, *i9* a 4, *i7* a 3, *i6* a 2, *i3* a 5, *h7* a 6, *g7* an 8, *g1* a 3, *h1* a 2, *g3* a 4, *b3* an 8, *c3* a 9, *c1* a 5, *g6* a 6, *g4* a 5, *e1* a 9, *c7* a 2, *f7* a 5, *d7* a 4, *e9* a 7, *c5* a 4, *c6* a 1, *c9* a 6, *d9* an 8, *f9* a 9, *b9* a 1, *b8* a 5, *d1* a 6, *f1* an 8, *b6* a 3, *h6* a 4, *h4* a 3, *b5* a 2, *b4* a 6, *f5* a 3, *d5* a 5, *f3* a 2, *f8* a 6, *d4* a 2, *e4* a 4, *d8* a 3, *e8* a 2, *d3* a 7, and *e3* a 3.

Answers

(Answer keys marked with a * indicate puzzles for which complete step-by-step solving instructions are available immediately following puzzle #100.)

1*

8	1	7	4	6	3	9	2	5
2	5	4	1	9	7	3	8	6
9	3	6	8	2	5	1	4	7
6	7	9	5	8	4	2	1	3
1	4	8	3	7	2	5	6	9
5	2	3	6	1	9	4	7	8
3	8	5	2	4	6	7	9	1
4	9	1	7	3	8	6	5	2
7	6	2	9	5	1	8	3	4

2*

1	6	9	7	5	2	3	8	4
3	2	4	8	1	6	5	7	9
7	5	8	3	4	9	1	2	6
8	4	6	5	9	3	7	1	2
9	1	2	4	8	7	6	3	5
5	3	7	2	6	1	9	4	8
4	8	1	9	3	5	2	6	7
6	7	5	1	2	4	8	9	3
2	9	3	6	7	8	4	5	1

3

5	1	7	3	8	6	2	9	4
3	6	8	4	9	2	5	7	1
2	4	9	7	1	5	8	6	3
9	8	2	6	4	1	3	5	7
4	5	1	2	3	7	9	8	6
6	7	3	9	5	8	4	1	2
8	3	5	1	6	4	7	2	9
1	2	4	5	7	9	6	3	8
7	9	6	8	2	3	1	4	5

4

2	9	8	1	3	5	6	7	4
6	7	1	9	8	4	3	5	2
4	5	3	7	6	2	8	9	1
5	1	2	4	9	8	7	3	6
7	3	4	5	2	6	1	8	9
9	8	6	3	7	1	4	2	5
1	6	7	8	5	9	2	4	3
3	2	9	6	4	7	5	1	8
8	4	5	2	1	3	9	6	7

5

7	5	1	4	9	8	6	3	2
4	6	2	1	3	7	5	9	8
9	3	8	6	5	2	7	1	4
5	8	6	2	4	3	1	7	9
2	9	3	7	6	1	8	4	5
1	7	4	9	8	5	3	2	6
6	1	7	8	2	9	4	5	3
3	4	9	5	7	6	2	8	1
8	2	5	3	1	4	9	6	7

6

6	3	5	4	7	9	2	8	1
9	8	1	2	6	5	3	4	7
2	7	4	3	8	1	9	6	5
4	9	6	7	5	8	1	2	3
3	5	8	1	9	2	4	7	6
1	2	7	6	3	4	8	5	9
8	1	3	5	2	7	6	9	4
7	4	9	8	1	6	5	3	2
5	6	2	9	4	3	7	1	8

7

5	3	9	7	2	1	4	8	6
1	4	2	8	5	6	3	9	7
7	8	6	4	3	9	2	1	5
2	6	8	5	9	4	1	7	3
3	9	5	1	7	8	6	2	4
4	7	1	2	6	3	9	5	8
8	5	4	6	1	2	7	3	9
6	2	3	9	8	7	5	4	1
9	1	7	3	4	5	8	6	2

8

6	2	3	5	1	9	8	4	7
4	5	7	3	8	6	2	9	1
9	8	1	4	7	2	6	3	5
8	9	4	6	3	1	7	5	2
1	6	5	2	4	7	9	8	3
7	3	2	8	9	5	4	1	6
2	1	6	9	5	8	3	7	4
3	7	8	1	6	4	5	2	9
5	4	9	7	2	3	1	6	8

9

6	1	2	8	7	9	3	4	5
8	3	7	5	1	4	9	2	6
4	9	5	2	6	3	8	7	1
7	5	4	3	9	6	2	1	8
9	2	1	4	5	8	6	3	7
3	8	6	7	2	1	4	5	9
5	6	3	9	4	7	1	8	2
1	7	8	6	3	2	5	9	4
2	4	9	1	8	5	7	6	3

10

4	7	2	9	5	3	1	8	6
8	3	6	1	7	2	5	9	4
1	9	5	8	4	6	3	2	7
2	1	7	4	8	9	6	3	5
3	5	8	7	6	1	2	4	9
6	4	9	2	3	5	7	1	8
5	2	4	3	9	7	8	6	1
7	8	3	6	1	4	9	5	2
9	6	1	5	2	8	4	7	3

11

3	6	1	4	9	8	7	2	5
9	5	8	2	7	6	1	4	3
4	7	2	1	3	5	8	9	6
5	8	4	7	1	9	6	3	2
1	2	3	6	5	4	9	8	7
6	9	7	3	8	2	5	1	4
7	3	5	9	2	1	4	6	8
2	4	9	8	6	7	3	5	1
8	1	6	5	4	3	2	7	9

12

9	3	5	2	4	7	1	8	6
2	8	6	3	1	9	4	5	7
4	7	1	5	6	8	9	3	2
8	1	2	4	7	6	5	9	3
7	4	3	9	2	5	6	1	8
5	6	9	1	8	3	2	7	4
1	5	7	6	3	4	8	2	9
3	9	4	8	5	2	7	6	1
6	2	8	7	9	1	3	4	5

13

7	4	5	8	9	2	3	1	6
1	2	3	6	5	7	9	4	8
9	6	8	3	4	1	7	2	5
5	8	7	9	1	6	4	3	2
2	3	9	4	8	5	1	6	7
6	1	4	7	2	3	5	8	9
4	7	2	5	3	8	6	9	1
8	9	6	1	7	4	2	5	3
3	5	1	2	6	9	8	7	4

14

8	9	6	5	7	4	3	1	2
3	7	4	1	9	2	8	5	6
1	2	5	3	6	8	7	4	9
6	3	1	8	2	7	5	9	4
7	4	9	6	5	1	2	8	3
5	8	2	4	3	9	6	7	1
9	5	7	2	1	3	4	6	8
2	1	8	7	4	6	9	3	5
4	6	3	9	8	5	1	2	7

15

7	1	9	6	4	8	5	2	3
5	6	8	3	7	2	1	9	4
3	2	4	1	5	9	8	6	7
6	4	1	9	8	5	3	7	2
8	7	3	2	6	1	4	5	9
2	9	5	4	3	7	6	1	8
9	8	6	7	1	4	2	3	5
4	3	7	5	2	6	9	8	1
1	5	2	8	9	3	7	4	6

16

8	3	2	1	9	7	6	4	5
1	6	7	2	4	5	9	8	3
4	9	5	8	6	3	2	7	1
5	8	6	4	1	2	3	9	7
9	2	1	7	3	6	4	5	8
3	7	4	5	8	9	1	2	6
2	4	8	6	7	1	5	3	9
7	1	9	3	5	4	8	6	2
6	5	3	9	2	8	7	1	4

17

4	3	6	5	8	1	7	2	9
1	8	2	9	7	6	3	5	4
5	7	9	2	3	4	8	1	6
7	2	8	6	4	3	5	9	1
3	6	5	8	1	9	4	7	2
9	4	1	7	2	5	6	8	3
6	5	3	1	9	7	2	4	8
8	1	7	4	6	2	9	3	5
2	9	4	3	5	8	1	6	7

18

9	3	1	6	2	8	7	4	5
5	7	8	3	4	9	1	6	2
2	6	4	5	1	7	3	8	9
4	8	3	2	9	5	6	1	7
6	5	2	8	7	1	4	9	3
1	9	7	4	6	3	2	5	8
8	1	5	7	3	4	9	2	6
7	2	9	1	8	6	5	3	4
3	4	6	9	5	2	8	7	1

19

3	6	4	7	9	8	5	1	2
1	7	9	2	3	5	4	8	6
2	5	8	6	4	1	3	7	9
5	3	2	4	8	6	1	9	7
7	8	1	3	2	9	6	4	5
9	4	6	1	5	7	8	2	3
4	9	3	8	6	2	7	5	1
8	1	5	9	7	3	2	6	4
6	2	7	5	1	4	9	3	8

20

8	9	3	7	2	4	1	6	5
1	2	7	5	3	6	4	8	9
4	6	5	1	9	8	3	2	7
7	5	1	2	4	9	6	3	8
6	8	9	3	5	1	7	4	2
2	3	4	6	8	7	5	9	1
5	4	6	9	7	2	8	1	3
9	7	8	4	1	3	2	5	6
3	1	2	8	6	5	9	7	4

21

9	1	3	8	5	2	7	6	4
8	5	7	1	4	6	9	3	2
4	2	6	7	9	3	5	1	8
1	8	5	6	2	4	3	7	9
3	6	4	9	8	7	2	5	1
7	9	2	3	1	5	4	8	6
2	3	1	4	7	8	6	9	5
6	4	9	5	3	1	8	2	7
5	7	8	2	6	9	1	4	3

22

8	9	3	6	4	5	2	1	7
6	4	1	8	7	2	3	9	5
2	5	7	3	1	9	4	6	8
9	8	6	2	5	3	1	7	4
3	1	4	7	9	8	5	2	6
5	7	2	1	6	4	9	8	3
1	6	5	9	3	7	8	4	2
4	2	9	5	8	6	7	3	1
7	3	8	4	2	1	6	5	9

23

6	1	3	9	4	7	2	5	8
9	5	4	8	6	2	7	1	3
2	7	8	3	5	1	4	9	6
5	2	1	6	3	8	9	7	4
4	6	7	1	2	9	8	3	5
8	3	9	4	7	5	6	2	1
7	8	2	5	1	6	3	4	9
1	4	6	2	9	3	5	8	7
3	9	5	7	8	4	1	6	2

24

3	9	1	6	8	4	7	5	2
4	2	5	7	3	9	1	8	6
8	6	7	1	5	2	4	9	3
2	8	3	5	1	6	9	4	7
9	1	4	2	7	8	3	6	5
5	7	6	4	9	3	8	2	1
6	3	9	8	2	1	5	7	4
7	4	8	3	6	5	2	1	9
1	5	2	9	4	7	6	3	8

25

8	5	2	7	9	1	4	3	6
6	7	1	3	2	4	8	5	9
9	4	3	5	8	6	2	1	7
4	6	9	8	5	3	7	2	1
2	1	7	6	4	9	5	8	3
3	8	5	1	7	2	9	6	4
1	9	4	2	3	8	6	7	5
5	3	8	9	6	7	1	4	2
7	2	6	4	1	5	3	9	8

26*

5	3	2	1	4	8	6	9	7
7	8	4	9	6	5	3	2	1
1	6	9	2	7	3	4	5	8
3	1	7	5	2	6	8	4	9
4	9	6	8	3	7	5	1	2
2	5	8	4	1	9	7	6	3
9	2	3	6	8	4	1	7	5
6	7	5	3	9	1	2	8	4
8	4	1	7	5	2	9	3	6

27*

7	3	2	5	4	8	6	1	9
9	5	8	2	6	1	4	7	3
1	4	6	7	3	9	2	8	5
2	8	5	4	9	6	7	3	1
4	6	7	1	5	3	8	9	2
3	1	9	8	7	2	5	6	4
8	9	3	6	2	5	1	4	7
6	2	4	9	1	7	3	5	8
5	7	1	3	8	4	9	2	6

28

4	9	6	2	7	5	1	3	8
7	3	2	9	8	1	6	5	4
8	5	1	6	3	4	2	7	9
3	1	4	7	2	8	9	6	5
9	6	7	5	4	3	8	1	2
5	2	8	1	9	6	3	4	7
6	4	5	8	1	9	7	2	3
1	7	9	3	5	2	4	8	6
2	8	3	4	6	7	5	9	1

29

9	2	5	8	3	7	6	4	1
7	3	1	2	4	6	8	5	9
4	8	6	1	5	9	7	3	2
1	9	4	5	6	2	3	7	8
8	6	7	4	1	3	9	2	5
3	5	2	9	7	8	1	6	4
5	1	3	7	8	4	2	9	6
6	4	9	3	2	1	5	8	7
2	7	8	6	9	5	4	1	3

30

9	3	2	4	7	6	8	1	5
8	1	6	5	2	3	9	7	4
4	5	7	9	1	8	6	3	2
3	9	5	7	4	1	2	6	8
2	6	1	8	3	9	5	4	7
7	8	4	6	5	2	3	9	1
5	4	3	2	6	7	1	8	9
1	7	8	3	9	5	4	2	6
6	2	9	1	8	4	7	5	3

31

1	7	6	4	8	3	2	9	5
8	5	3	6	9	2	7	1	4
4	9	2	5	7	1	6	3	8
3	1	7	2	6	8	4	5	9
2	6	5	9	3	4	8	7	1
9	4	8	7	1	5	3	2	6
6	3	1	8	2	9	5	4	7
7	2	4	1	5	6	9	8	3
5	8	9	3	4	7	1	6	2

32

2	4	9	6	8	1	5	3	7
7	1	6	5	9	3	8	2	4
8	5	3	4	7	2	9	6	1
3	6	2	7	1	5	4	8	9
1	9	8	2	3	4	6	7	5
5	7	4	8	6	9	3	1	2
6	8	1	9	4	7	2	5	3
9	3	5	1	2	6	7	4	8
4	2	7	3	5	8	1	9	6

33

5	4	2	9	1	8	3	6	7
7	8	3	4	6	5	1	9	2
9	1	6	2	7	3	5	4	8
8	2	9	7	3	6	4	5	1
1	3	7	5	8	4	9	2	6
4	6	5	1	2	9	8	7	3
2	5	1	8	9	7	6	3	4
6	9	8	3	4	2	7	1	5
3	7	4	6	5	1	2	8	9

34

9	3	6	2	7	1	8	4	5
8	2	4	6	5	9	7	3	1
1	7	5	3	4	8	2	6	9
6	5	2	9	3	7	4	1	8
4	9	1	5	8	2	6	7	3
3	8	7	4	1	6	9	5	2
5	6	9	7	2	3	1	8	4
2	1	3	8	6	4	5	9	7
7	4	8	1	9	5	3	2	6

35

4	5	3	8	2	6	1	9	7
1	8	7	3	5	9	4	6	2
2	9	6	4	7	1	5	8	3
9	7	4	1	6	3	8	2	5
3	1	2	5	8	7	9	4	6
5	6	8	2	9	4	7	3	1
6	4	1	7	3	8	2	5	9
8	2	9	6	1	5	3	7	4
7	3	5	9	4	2	6	1	8

36

6	2	4	9	8	5	1	3	7
9	8	1	7	6	3	5	2	4
7	3	5	4	2	1	6	8	9
1	5	3	8	4	9	2	7	6
8	7	6	3	5	2	9	4	1
2	4	9	1	7	6	3	5	8
4	1	2	6	3	7	8	9	5
3	6	7	5	9	8	4	1	2
5	9	8	2	1	4	7	6	3

37

7	2	3	5	8	1	4	6	9
4	1	6	9	2	7	8	3	5
9	8	5	6	3	4	7	2	1
5	9	1	4	6	3	2	7	8
6	7	8	2	1	9	5	4	3
3	4	2	8	7	5	9	1	6
1	5	7	3	9	2	6	8	4
8	3	9	7	4	6	1	5	2
2	6	4	1	5	8	3	9	7

38

1	7	2	4	3	8	9	5	6
3	6	8	2	5	9	4	7	1
9	4	5	6	1	7	2	3	8
4	1	6	7	2	5	3	8	9
2	8	7	3	9	4	6	1	5
5	9	3	8	6	1	7	2	4
8	3	9	5	4	2	1	6	7
7	2	4	1	8	6	5	9	3
6	5	1	9	7	3	8	4	2

39

7	3	5	4	9	8	1	6	2
4	8	1	5	6	2	9	7	3
9	6	2	3	1	7	5	4	8
8	7	4	9	2	5	6	3	1
5	9	3	6	7	1	8	2	4
2	1	6	8	4	3	7	9	5
1	5	7	2	3	9	4	8	6
6	2	8	7	5	4	3	1	9
3	4	9	1	8	6	2	5	7

40

1	2	6	4	8	5	3	9	7
7	8	5	6	3	9	4	2	1
9	4	3	7	1	2	6	5	8
5	3	8	2	7	6	1	4	9
2	9	7	8	4	1	5	3	6
6	1	4	5	9	3	7	8	2
8	6	2	3	5	7	9	1	4
4	5	1	9	6	8	2	7	3
3	7	9	1	2	4	8	6	5

41

4	3	2	5	8	6	9	1	7
5	7	8	9	1	3	6	4	2
6	9	1	7	2	4	5	3	8
9	1	6	8	4	5	2	7	3
7	5	3	1	6	2	8	9	4
8	2	4	3	7	9	1	5	6
2	8	7	4	9	1	3	6	5
1	6	5	2	3	7	4	8	9
3	4	9	6	5	8	7	2	1

42

5	3	1	6	4	2	8	7	9
9	6	7	8	3	5	4	2	1
8	2	4	7	9	1	3	5	6
1	8	6	2	5	3	9	4	7
4	7	9	1	6	8	5	3	2
2	5	3	9	7	4	1	6	8
6	9	5	4	1	7	2	8	3
7	4	8	3	2	9	6	1	5
3	1	2	5	8	6	7	9	4

43

7	6	8	5	2	9	1	4	3
4	2	5	3	7	1	9	6	8
9	1	3	8	4	6	5	7	2
5	4	1	6	8	7	2	3	9
6	8	2	9	3	4	7	1	5
3	9	7	2	1	5	6	8	4
2	7	9	4	6	3	8	5	1
8	3	6	1	5	2	4	9	7
1	5	4	7	9	8	3	2	6

44

8	6	5	9	2	7	1	4	3
9	3	7	4	5	1	8	2	6
2	4	1	8	6	3	9	7	5
5	8	2	7	4	9	6	3	1
4	9	3	6	1	5	2	8	7
7	1	6	3	8	2	5	9	4
6	7	4	1	9	8	3	5	2
3	2	9	5	7	6	4	1	8
1	5	8	2	3	4	7	6	9

45

7	5	9	8	4	6	3	1	2
8	1	2	9	3	7	5	6	4
6	4	3	1	5	2	8	9	7
2	9	6	7	8	5	1	4	3
1	7	5	4	6	3	9	2	8
4	3	8	2	9	1	7	5	6
5	8	1	6	7	4	2	3	9
3	6	7	5	2	9	4	8	1
9	2	4	3	1	8	6	7	5

46

8	2	9	5	7	1	4	3	6
5	3	4	9	6	8	7	2	1
6	1	7	2	4	3	5	8	9
4	6	5	3	2	7	1	9	8
2	9	1	4	8	5	6	7	3
3	7	8	1	9	6	2	4	5
7	5	3	8	1	4	9	6	2
1	4	2	6	3	9	8	5	7
9	8	6	7	5	2	3	1	4

47

8	9	5	1	3	4	2	7	6
6	1	3	2	9	7	4	8	5
7	4	2	5	8	6	3	1	9
1	6	4	3	7	9	5	2	8
3	5	9	8	4	2	1	6	7
2	8	7	6	1	5	9	4	3
4	7	8	9	5	1	6	3	2
5	2	1	7	6	3	8	9	4
9	3	6	4	2	8	7	5	1

48

3	8	7	4	5	6	9	2	1
4	1	9	8	2	3	6	5	7
6	2	5	1	7	9	4	8	3
5	6	8	2	1	7	3	9	4
9	7	4	5	3	8	1	6	2
2	3	1	9	6	4	5	7	8
1	9	2	3	8	5	7	4	6
8	5	6	7	4	1	2	3	9
7	4	3	6	9	2	8	1	5

49

9	5	2	4	3	6	7	8	1
1	4	3	8	7	2	6	9	5
6	8	7	5	9	1	4	3	2
7	3	4	9	2	5	1	6	8
5	6	8	3	1	7	9	2	4
2	1	9	6	8	4	5	7	3
8	7	6	1	5	3	2	4	9
4	9	5	2	6	8	3	1	7
3	2	1	7	4	9	8	5	6

50

3	6	2	7	4	5	1	8	9
9	7	4	2	1	8	5	3	6
1	5	8	3	6	9	4	7	2
7	1	9	6	5	2	8	4	3
2	4	6	1	8	3	7	9	5
5	8	3	4	9	7	6	2	1
6	9	1	8	3	4	2	5	7
8	2	5	9	7	1	3	6	4
4	3	7	5	2	6	9	1	8

51*

5	8	7	4	6	1	2	9	3
2	1	4	9	7	3	8	5	6
9	3	6	2	8	5	7	1	4
8	6	3	1	4	9	5	2	7
4	9	5	8	2	7	6	3	1
1	7	2	3	5	6	9	4	8
6	2	8	5	1	4	3	7	9
7	4	9	6	3	2	1	8	5
3	5	1	7	9	8	4	6	2

52*

6	7	2	5	8	4	3	1	9
9	8	3	6	1	7	5	2	4
1	4	5	2	9	3	7	6	8
2	5	9	1	3	8	4	7	6
4	6	1	7	2	9	8	3	5
7	3	8	4	6	5	1	9	2
5	1	7	9	4	2	6	8	3
3	2	4	8	7	6	9	5	1
8	9	6	3	5	1	2	4	7

53

7	3	2	4	8	6	1	5	9
5	1	8	9	2	3	6	4	7
6	9	4	7	1	5	2	3	8
8	4	5	6	9	1	3	7	2
1	7	3	2	5	8	4	9	6
9	2	6	3	7	4	8	1	5
3	5	7	8	4	2	9	6	1
4	8	1	5	6	9	7	2	3
2	6	9	1	3	7	5	8	4

54

8	3	2	4	6	9	1	7	5
1	9	6	5	7	8	2	4	3
7	5	4	3	1	2	8	9	6
5	2	1	7	4	6	9	3	8
6	8	7	1	9	3	4	5	2
3	4	9	8	2	5	6	1	7
9	1	8	6	3	7	5	2	4
4	7	5	2	8	1	3	6	9
2	6	3	9	5	4	7	8	1

55

7	6	2	9	4	5	1	8	3
4	3	8	7	2	1	6	5	9
9	1	5	3	6	8	7	2	4
5	2	4	1	3	7	8	9	6
8	7	6	5	9	4	2	3	1
1	9	3	2	8	6	5	4	7
2	5	9	6	7	3	4	1	8
3	4	7	8	1	2	9	6	5
6	8	1	4	5	9	3	7	2

56

8	5	7	6	4	3	9	2	1
4	2	3	1	7	9	5	6	8
9	1	6	2	5	8	3	4	7
7	8	9	5	2	6	4	1	3
2	3	1	7	9	4	6	8	5
5	6	4	8	3	1	7	9	2
3	4	8	9	1	7	2	5	6
6	9	5	3	8	2	1	7	4
1	7	2	4	6	5	8	3	9

57

7	9	6	4	3	5	1	8	2
4	3	8	2	6	1	9	5	7
1	2	5	7	9	8	6	3	4
3	5	1	6	7	9	2	4	8
8	4	9	3	5	2	7	6	1
2	6	7	1	8	4	5	9	3
9	1	3	5	4	7	8	2	6
6	8	2	9	1	3	4	7	5
5	7	4	8	2	6	3	1	9

58

2	8	4	3	7	1	6	5	9
5	1	9	8	2	6	3	4	7
3	6	7	4	5	9	1	2	8
6	3	5	2	4	8	9	7	1
8	4	1	9	6	7	2	3	5
7	9	2	5	1	3	4	8	6
9	2	3	6	8	5	7	1	4
1	5	6	7	3	4	8	9	2
4	7	8	1	9	2	5	6	3

59

3	4	2	5	6	1	9	7	8
6	5	8	2	9	7	3	1	4
9	1	7	4	3	8	6	2	5
7	9	5	6	4	3	2	8	1
1	6	3	7	8	2	4	5	9
8	2	4	1	5	9	7	3	6
5	3	1	9	7	6	8	4	2
2	8	6	3	1	4	5	9	7
4	7	9	8	2	5	1	6	3

60

3	9	7	6	1	2	5	4	8
8	5	1	9	3	4	7	6	2
4	6	2	8	5	7	1	3	9
2	8	3	5	7	1	4	9	6
6	7	5	4	9	3	8	2	1
9	1	4	2	8	6	3	5	7
1	3	9	7	6	5	2	8	4
5	4	8	1	2	9	6	7	3
7	2	6	3	4	8	9	1	5

61

6	8	9	4	2	7	3	5	1
2	3	7	5	6	1	4	8	9
4	5	1	3	8	9	7	2	6
3	1	4	2	5	6	9	7	8
5	7	6	8	9	4	2	1	3
8	9	2	7	1	3	5	6	4
9	2	8	1	4	5	6	3	7
1	6	3	9	7	2	8	4	5
7	4	5	6	3	8	1	9	2

62

8	1	3	5	7	2	9	6	4
4	7	2	6	3	9	5	8	1
9	6	5	8	1	4	2	3	7
3	4	6	7	9	1	8	2	5
1	9	7	2	5	8	3	4	6
2	5	8	4	6	3	1	7	9
6	2	9	3	4	5	7	1	8
7	3	1	9	8	6	4	5	2
5	8	4	1	2	7	6	9	3

63

7	4	5	3	8	6	1	9	2
1	8	9	5	2	4	7	3	6
6	3	2	1	9	7	5	4	8
5	9	4	8	6	1	2	7	3
8	6	3	9	7	2	4	5	1
2	1	7	4	5	3	6	8	9
4	5	8	6	1	9	3	2	7
9	7	6	2	3	5	8	1	4
3	2	1	7	4	8	9	6	5

64

2	7	1	9	5	8	6	3	4
8	6	3	1	4	2	7	5	9
5	4	9	3	6	7	8	1	2
4	5	7	2	1	6	3	9	8
3	1	6	5	8	9	4	2	7
9	2	8	7	3	4	5	6	1
7	9	4	6	2	3	1	8	5
6	8	5	4	9	1	2	7	3
1	3	2	8	7	5	9	4	6

65

6	7	9	1	2	5	3	8	4
5	3	1	9	8	4	2	7	6
4	2	8	3	6	7	5	1	9
3	4	6	7	9	2	8	5	1
7	1	2	6	5	8	4	9	3
8	9	5	4	3	1	7	6	2
9	5	4	2	7	6	1	3	8
2	8	3	5	1	9	6	4	7
1	6	7	8	4	3	9	2	5

66

3	2	8	7	4	9	1	5	6
7	6	9	5	1	2	8	3	4
1	4	5	6	3	8	9	7	2
8	9	4	1	5	3	2	6	7
6	5	3	9	2	7	4	1	8
2	1	7	4	8	6	3	9	5
9	8	2	3	7	5	6	4	1
5	3	1	8	6	4	7	2	9
4	7	6	2	9	1	5	8	3

67

7	9	6	3	5	2	1	8	4
8	3	2	1	9	4	6	5	7
4	1	5	7	8	6	3	9	2
1	8	3	9	4	7	5	2	6
5	7	9	6	2	3	4	1	8
2	6	4	5	1	8	9	7	3
9	4	7	8	6	1	2	3	5
6	5	8	2	3	9	7	4	1
3	2	1	4	7	5	8	6	9

68

9	1	4	7	3	8	2	5	6
6	5	8	2	4	1	9	7	3
3	2	7	9	5	6	4	8	1
5	7	3	6	1	4	8	9	2
8	4	9	3	7	2	1	6	5
2	6	1	5	8	9	3	4	7
1	3	6	8	9	5	7	2	4
7	9	2	4	6	3	5	1	8
4	8	5	1	2	7	6	3	9

69

2	8	6	3	7	1	9	4	5
4	7	9	2	5	6	1	8	3
1	5	3	4	9	8	6	2	7
8	4	2	7	6	3	5	1	9
3	6	5	8	1	9	4	7	2
9	1	7	5	4	2	8	3	6
6	9	4	1	3	7	2	5	8
7	2	1	6	8	5	3	9	4
5	3	8	9	2	4	7	6	1

70

8	3	4	1	5	9	2	6	7
1	6	2	4	7	8	9	3	5
5	9	7	6	2	3	8	4	1
7	2	1	3	9	4	6	5	8
9	5	6	2	8	7	4	1	3
3	4	8	5	6	1	7	2	9
6	1	9	7	3	2	5	8	4
2	8	3	9	4	5	1	7	6
4	7	5	8	1	6	3	9	2

71

1	2	3	5	4	6	7	9	8
7	6	9	1	2	8	4	5	3
5	8	4	7	9	3	1	2	6
4	3	6	9	7	2	5	8	1
2	9	1	6	8	5	3	7	4
8	5	7	4	3	1	2	6	9
3	1	5	2	6	9	8	4	7
6	4	2	8	1	7	9	3	5
9	7	8	3	5	4	6	1	2

72

2	4	7	8	1	6	5	3	9
9	8	5	3	2	7	6	1	4
3	1	6	4	9	5	2	8	7
8	6	3	1	4	2	9	7	5
1	7	2	5	3	9	8	4	6
5	9	4	7	6	8	3	2	1
7	5	9	2	8	1	4	6	3
4	2	1	6	5	3	7	9	8
6	3	8	9	7	4	1	5	2

73

9	1	7	6	3	8	4	5	2
8	3	2	1	5	4	6	9	7
4	5	6	2	9	7	1	8	3
3	6	9	4	2	1	5	7	8
2	4	8	5	7	6	3	1	9
1	7	5	9	8	3	2	6	4
5	2	4	8	1	9	7	3	6
6	9	3	7	4	5	8	2	1
7	8	1	3	6	2	9	4	5

74

6	9	4	5	8	2	1	3	7
7	1	2	9	6	3	5	8	4
8	5	3	4	1	7	9	2	6
3	6	7	2	4	9	8	1	5
1	4	8	6	3	5	7	9	2
5	2	9	8	7	1	6	4	3
2	3	6	7	9	8	4	5	1
4	8	5	1	2	6	3	7	9
9	7	1	3	5	4	2	6	8

75

9	4	5	3	7	2	1	6	8
2	6	8	9	4	1	5	3	7
7	1	3	8	6	5	9	2	4
4	3	2	1	5	8	6	7	9
5	9	7	2	3	6	4	8	1
6	8	1	4	9	7	3	5	2
1	5	6	7	2	4	8	9	3
3	2	4	5	8	9	7	1	6
8	7	9	6	1	3	2	4	5

76*

4	2	7	6	3	5	9	8	1
5	6	1	9	8	7	3	4	2
3	9	8	1	2	4	5	6	7
8	4	3	7	6	9	2	1	5
6	7	2	8	5	1	4	3	9
9	1	5	2	4	3	6	7	8
1	8	4	3	9	2	7	5	6
2	5	6	4	7	8	1	9	3
7	3	9	5	1	6	8	2	4

77

3	6	1	7	5	9	8	4	2
2	9	7	1	8	4	6	5	3
4	5	8	2	3	6	1	9	7
5	7	4	9	1	3	2	6	8
6	3	9	4	2	8	7	1	5
1	8	2	5	6	7	4	3	9
8	1	6	3	7	5	9	2	4
7	4	5	6	9	2	3	8	1
9	2	3	8	4	1	5	7	6

78

8	1	6	3	7	5	9	2	4
5	7	2	4	8	9	6	1	3
3	4	9	1	6	2	8	7	5
6	3	8	7	5	4	2	9	1
4	2	7	8	9	1	5	3	6
9	5	1	2	3	6	7	4	8
2	9	5	6	1	3	4	8	7
1	8	4	5	2	7	3	6	9
7	6	3	9	4	8	1	5	2

79

4	2	7	3	8	9	5	6	1
6	9	1	7	5	4	3	2	8
3	5	8	2	1	6	7	4	9
2	6	5	8	4	7	9	1	3
1	7	9	5	6	3	2	8	4
8	4	3	1	9	2	6	7	5
7	8	2	4	3	5	1	9	6
5	1	6	9	7	8	4	3	2
9	3	4	6	2	1	8	5	7

80

9	4	3	6	1	5	7	2	8
2	8	1	3	7	9	4	6	5
5	6	7	4	2	8	1	9	3
6	5	8	2	3	4	9	1	7
7	2	9	5	8	1	6	3	4
3	1	4	9	6	7	5	8	2
8	3	5	7	9	6	2	4	1
1	7	6	8	4	2	3	5	9
4	9	2	1	5	3	8	7	6

81

5	8	1	7	6	3	2	9	4
4	2	6	8	9	1	5	3	7
9	3	7	4	2	5	6	8	1
1	7	5	3	8	4	9	2	6
6	4	3	9	1	2	7	5	8
8	9	2	6	5	7	4	1	3
7	5	4	2	3	8	1	6	9
3	1	9	5	4	6	8	7	2
2	6	8	1	7	9	3	4	5

82

9	2	5	4	8	1	6	7	3
6	7	1	2	3	9	4	5	8
3	8	4	5	7	6	9	1	2
1	4	7	3	5	2	8	6	9
8	6	2	9	1	7	5	3	4
5	3	9	6	4	8	7	2	1
2	1	6	7	9	4	3	8	5
4	5	8	1	6	3	2	9	7
7	9	3	8	2	5	1	4	6

83

2	3	1	9	8	5	6	4	7
8	9	7	6	3	4	5	1	2
4	6	5	2	7	1	3	8	9
3	8	9	1	5	6	7	2	4
1	2	4	7	9	3	8	5	6
5	7	6	8	4	2	9	3	1
9	5	2	4	6	8	1	7	3
6	1	3	5	2	7	4	9	8
7	4	8	3	1	9	2	6	5

84

9	3	5	1	8	7	6	4	2
1	4	8	2	6	5	7	9	3
7	2	6	3	9	4	1	5	8
5	1	9	8	7	6	2	3	4
2	8	3	5	4	1	9	7	6
4	6	7	9	2	3	5	8	1
8	7	1	4	5	2	3	6	9
3	5	4	6	1	9	8	2	7
6	9	2	7	3	8	4	1	5

85

7	8	5	6	4	9	1	3	2
6	4	3	5	1	2	7	9	8
1	9	2	8	7	3	4	5	6
2	3	8	7	6	4	5	1	9
5	7	6	3	9	1	8	2	4
9	1	4	2	8	5	3	6	7
4	6	1	9	5	7	2	8	3
3	5	9	4	2	8	6	7	1
8	2	7	1	3	6	9	4	5

86

1	3	6	8	7	2	4	9	5
2	8	5	9	1	4	7	3	6
4	7	9	5	3	6	2	1	8
6	4	3	1	2	9	5	8	7
7	2	8	4	5	3	1	6	9
9	5	1	7	6	8	3	4	2
5	1	4	6	8	7	9	2	3
3	6	7	2	9	1	8	5	4
8	9	2	3	4	5	6	7	1

87

2	4	3	8	7	9	5	6	1
9	5	8	6	1	4	2	7	3
7	6	1	3	5	2	4	9	8
1	7	4	9	2	6	3	8	5
5	3	6	1	4	8	7	2	9
8	9	2	5	3	7	6	1	4
3	1	7	2	8	5	9	4	6
4	8	9	7	6	3	1	5	2
6	2	5	4	9	1	8	3	7

88

9	5	4	7	2	3	8	6	1
2	1	8	5	6	9	4	7	3
3	6	7	4	1	8	5	9	2
5	4	9	2	7	1	3	8	6
7	2	3	6	8	5	1	4	9
6	8	1	9	3	4	7	2	5
4	7	5	1	9	6	2	3	8
8	9	2	3	5	7	6	1	4
1	3	6	8	4	2	9	5	7

89

3	9	1	6	2	5	4	8	7
6	7	8	3	1	4	9	5	2
5	4	2	9	8	7	1	6	3
7	6	4	1	5	8	2	3	9
2	5	9	7	4	3	8	1	6
1	8	3	2	9	6	7	4	5
9	2	5	4	6	1	3	7	8
8	1	7	5	3	9	6	2	4
4	3	6	8	7	2	5	9	1

90

6	7	1	9	5	2	4	8	3
3	5	2	4	1	8	6	9	7
9	8	4	7	6	3	5	2	1
4	1	9	6	2	5	3	7	8
5	6	3	8	7	1	9	4	2
7	2	8	3	9	4	1	6	5
2	4	5	1	8	9	7	3	6
8	3	7	5	4	6	2	1	9
1	9	6	2	3	7	8	5	4

91

4	8	1	3	2	5	7	9	6
7	3	6	9	8	1	2	4	5
5	9	2	4	6	7	8	3	1
9	5	3	6	7	4	1	8	2
6	2	4	5	1	8	3	7	9
8	1	7	2	9	3	5	6	4
1	4	5	8	3	9	6	2	7
2	7	8	1	4	6	9	5	3
3	6	9	7	5	2	4	1	8

92

4	5	1	3	2	7	9	8	6
3	2	7	6	9	8	5	1	4
8	6	9	4	5	1	2	7	3
6	1	2	8	3	9	4	5	7
9	4	5	7	1	2	6	3	8
7	8	3	5	6	4	1	9	2
1	7	4	9	8	6	3	2	5
5	9	8	2	4	3	7	6	1
2	3	6	1	7	5	8	4	9

93

8	3	1	7	5	6	9	4	2
5	9	6	4	2	1	8	3	7
7	2	4	9	3	8	5	6	1
2	1	5	3	8	4	7	9	6
9	6	3	1	7	2	4	5	8
4	8	7	6	9	5	1	2	3
1	7	2	5	4	3	6	8	9
3	5	9	8	6	7	2	1	4
6	4	8	2	1	9	3	7	5

94

1	3	5	4	9	6	7	2	8
4	6	7	8	3	2	5	9	1
9	2	8	5	7	1	3	6	4
8	5	6	2	1	7	9	4	3
7	4	9	3	8	5	6	1	2
2	1	3	9	6	4	8	7	5
6	9	2	1	5	3	4	8	7
3	7	1	6	4	8	2	5	9
5	8	4	7	2	9	1	3	6

95

7	4	2	6	1	5	9	8	3
1	8	3	2	9	7	5	4	6
5	6	9	8	4	3	2	1	7
4	3	8	7	5	1	6	2	9
2	7	6	4	8	9	1	3	5
9	1	5	3	6	2	4	7	8
3	9	7	5	2	4	8	6	1
8	2	1	9	7	6	3	5	4
6	5	4	1	3	8	7	9	2

96

9	4	7	5	8	2	6	1	3
5	6	3	4	1	7	8	9	2
8	1	2	6	9	3	7	4	5
6	7	8	2	5	9	1	3	4
2	3	5	1	4	6	9	7	8
4	9	1	7	3	8	5	2	6
3	8	6	9	2	1	4	5	7
7	5	9	3	6	4	2	8	1
1	2	4	8	7	5	3	6	9

97

7	5	9	6	8	1	4	2	3
1	8	2	3	5	4	7	6	9
3	4	6	9	2	7	5	8	1
5	3	4	1	7	6	2	9	8
9	1	8	2	3	5	6	7	4
2	6	7	4	9	8	3	1	5
4	2	3	8	6	9	1	5	7
8	7	1	5	4	2	9	3	6
6	9	5	7	1	3	8	4	2

98

7	1	5	6	4	2	3	8	9
9	2	4	8	1	3	6	7	5
6	8	3	7	5	9	1	4	2
2	4	6	3	7	8	5	9	1
1	5	7	4	9	6	2	3	8
8	3	9	1	2	5	7	6	4
3	9	2	5	6	4	8	1	7
4	7	8	2	3	1	9	5	6
5	6	1	9	8	7	4	2	3

99

7	9	3	2	4	6	8	1	5
4	8	1	5	7	9	2	6	3
2	6	5	3	1	8	9	7	4
3	5	6	9	2	4	7	8	1
1	4	7	6	8	3	5	2	9
8	2	9	7	5	1	4	3	6
5	3	2	4	6	7	1	9	8
9	1	4	8	3	2	6	5	7
6	7	8	1	9	5	3	4	2

100*

1	2	6	8	9	5	7	4	3
4	7	8	6	2	3	9	5	1
5	3	9	7	4	1	2	8	6
6	1	7	2	5	9	4	3	8
9	5	3	4	6	8	1	2	7
8	4	2	1	3	7	5	6	9
3	9	4	5	1	6	8	7	2
2	8	1	3	7	4	6	9	5
7	6	5	9	8	2	3	1	4

Printed in Great Britain
by Amazon